THE WYSIS WAY

Offa's Dyke to The Thames Path

*'In Gloucestershire the hills aren't high,
They don't shut out the earth from the sky;
But they feed the Severn, the Thames and the Wye
Which no other hills can do.'*

Designed and compiled by Gerry Stewart
Illustrations by Genny Proctor

COUNTRYSIDE MATTERS

First published in 1997 by
COUNTRYSIDE MATTERS
15 Orchard Road
Alderton
Tewkesbury
Gloucestershire   GL20 8 NS

Typeset by Ex Libris Press
Bradford on Avon, Wiltshire

Printed and bound by Cromwell Press
Broughton Gifford, Melksham

ISBN 0 9527870 1 6

Contents

Acknowledgements   5

Credits   6

Introduction   7

Monmouth to Nailbridge – 12 miles   9

Nailbridge to Barbers Bridge – 121/2 miles   23

Barbers Bridge to Painswick Beacon – 121/2 miles   38

Painswick Beacon to Sapperton – 11 miles   53

Sapperton to Kemble – 53/4 miles   68

Mileage Chart   77

Tourist Information Centres   79

Author's Note

It should be recognised that changes continually take place in the countryside. Hedges disappear, new fences, sometimes without stiles or gates, arise and paths may be difficult to follow through crops. Additionally, public rights of way are subject to legal diversions which may not be reflected in current maps. County Council signposting should reveal these changes but the situation may not always be clear on the ground.

Whilst every possible care has been taken to ensure that the information provided in this guide book is accurate, neither the author nor publisher can accept responsibility for any errors or omissions or for the interpretation of the information by users of this guide book.

Acknowledgements

In 1990 the Gloucestershire Area of the Ramblers Association produced the outline of a Recreational Footpath across the county, linking the River Wye at Monmouth, with the Thames at Kemble.

The Ramblers were anxious to avoid a route, suggested by the County Council, with much of its length along the banks of the River Severn and the Thames and Severn Canal. It was felt that this route did not reflect the varied countryside in the county, particularly the diverse areas between the valleys of the Wye, Severn and Thames.

The main consideration was the provision of a varied route through pleasant countryside likely to appeal to walkers, from both home and abroad, who take pleasure from following a long continuous way on foot. Additionally, it was recognised that the route would form part of the network of long distance paths and should therefore link with major routes within the county.

Having produced a worthwhile route for consideration and deliberating at length on a suitable title, the Ramblers allowed their report to gather dust in the County Council's archives.

A few years later, while researching and writing up *The Gloucestershire Way*, I acknowledged the sections shared with the proposed route from Monmouth. From the summit of May Hill, pre-eminent Gloucestershire landmark, the concept of a route connecting the National Trails of Wales with the Thames Path was very appealing. Hopefully, the merits of the route will be confirmed when The Wysis Way becomes more widely known.

My wife Kate showed a good deal of fortitude during the very wintry week at Christmas 1996. Mid-winter car shuttles along ice-bound roads were not conducive to writing up enjoyable walking, and the slow and chilly daily progress tested her patience sorely. I am also grateful for her contribution in meticulously correcting drafts and advice when 'the wood couldn't be seen for the trees'.

The illustrations are partly the work of Hilary Jayne and my daughter Genny Proctor. My thanks to them for their respective efforts, particularly in working up my finicky design for the book cover.

Lastly, I have to mention Jim Davies of Swindon Ramblers. He had the temerity to write to me pointing out some necessary corrections to *The Gloucestershire Way*, for his trouble he was co-opted to walk over the route of The Wysis Way and check the text for accuracy. However, he is not to be held to blame for any slight errors which might be found.

Credits

The publishers wish to express their thanks for the use of the following poems to illustrate the countryside traversed by the Wysis Way. While every effort has been made to contact all copyright holders, the publishers would be pleased to hear from anyone whom they have been unable to trace.

Penny Ely, Trustee of the Gurney Estate, for 'The Old City' and 'Near Midsummer', by Ivor Gurney from *The Collected Poems of Ivor Gurney*. Patrick Harvey, for 'Devil's Chapel', by F.W. Harvey, from *A Gloucestershire Lad at Home and Abroad*. Andrew Dalby, for 'Springtime in December', by Arthur Dalby. Jeff Cooper, for 'Ryton Firs', by Lascelles Abercrombie, from *Twelve Idylls*. U.A. Fanthorpe and the Peterloo Poets, for 'On buying Sheet 163', from *Standing To*. The Society of Authors, as the Literary Representative of the Estate of John Masefield, for 'The Everlasting Mercy', from *The Collected Poems*. Pamela Haines, for 'Paradise', by John Haines, from *Poems*. The Literary Executor of the Estate of Frank Mansell, for 'Cotswold Choice', from *Cotswold Ballads*. Samuel French Ltd. as the Literary Representative of John Drinkwater, for 'Legacy', from *Tides*.

Introduction

The Wysis Way links two major National Trails, providing continuous walking for 400 miles from North Wales to the capital. Throughout this length, there are links with other National Trails and long distance paths as well as Britain's only, to date, Euro Route.

Built to the order of Offa, the powerful king of Mercia (the English Midlands), in 800 AD, the ancient earthwork of Offa's Dyke runs north – south through the Welsh Marches. Along the best preserved sections, the Dyke consists of a bank about 8 metres in height, often with an accompanying ditch, of comparable size. There is no historical record of the construction, and archaeologists are not agreed as to its purpose, whether intended to mark the boundary of his kingdom to the east or as a defensive structure, perhaps once capped by a stockade. The Dyke remains a tremendous achievement and memorial to Offa.

Opened in 1971, between Prestatyn on the North Wales coast, and Chepstow, on the border between Gwent and Gloucestershire, the Offa's Dyke Path National Trail is a fine accompaniment to this impressive national monument. For over half its 168 miles, the Trail keeps company with the Dyke, although this, in places, may be no more than a hedgebank or slight rise in a ploughed field.

Offa's Dyke Path meets and crosses the River Wye at Monmouth, from where The Wysis Way provides a link, through the attractive Gloucestershire countryside, to the Thames Path, the most recently designated National Trail. At Gloucester, the Severn Way, a 200 mile route from the source, on the Welsh hills, to the sea, is also joined.

Not always found in the same spot, but in one field or another just to the east of Kemble on the Gloucestershire wolds, the infant Thames, or Isis, rises from the limestone. To walk anywhere beside the Thames is to walk through English history, and long before Offa built his earthwork in the west, the Thames waterway was a trade route for both the

7

inhabitants and subsequent invaders. The ancient Dyke, whatever the reason for its construction, contrasts vividly with the medieval cloisters of Oxford, the Royal Palaces of Windsor, Hampton and Greenwich, and the engineering feat of the Thames Barrage.

Although a continuous Thameside path, much of it already in use for centuries, had been mooted for many years, only in 1996 was the Thames Path opened by the Countryside Commission as the latest National Trail. From Thameshead, where the Wysis Way ends, path and river meander for 180 miles to the Thames Barrier. The Thames Path is unique, for the present, in being the only National Trail following a river throughout its length.

The Severn is Britain's longest river. Rising in the mountains of mid Wales, close to the source of the Wye, the two rivers enclose countryside as pleasant and attractive as any in the country. The first section of the Wysis Way from Monmouth, traverses a tract of the Forest of Dean and the Leaden Vale which fully validates the old line, 'blessed is the eye between Severn and Wye'.

Although never as important as the Thames, the Severn was, nonetheless, a crucial trade route for the Midlands, for centuries. In 1701 there was a regular water taxi between Shrewsbury and Gloucester and by the middle of the 18th Century, 100,000 tons of coal was shipped from Coalport annually. Severn Trows of up to 80 tons laden, plied with the adjacent Midland towns, and downstream to the Bristol Channel ports and beyond. Although a good deal of bow hauling was involved, both by men and horses, because of strong tides and fresh water flow Severn traffic relied far less on towing than did Thames craft.

A long distance path, of 220 miles, has been planned along the Severn for several years. In 1989 a length of 50 miles on the east bank in Gloucestershire, was opened as the Severn Way. More recently, a continuous route has been created, alongside or near the river, through Worcestershire and Shropshire. A path along the higher reaches in Powys, through Newtown, Welshpool and Llandiloes, to the source on Plynlimon, will shortly become available.

Monmouth - Nailbridge

Monmouth once the county seat of Monmouthshire, is an attractive market and border town at the confluence of the rivers Wye and its tributary, the Monnow. Although used by the Romans, the continuous history of Monmouth began with the Normans as an easily defended site. They built the Castle in the 11th Century as the centre of a military, commercial and religious settlement. King Henry V was born there in 1387 and his statue adorns Agincourt Square.

The 13th century bridge over the Monnow is unique with a fortified gatehouse. Probably constructed for defence it was also used as a medieval toll house. The breadth of Monnow Street reflects its use as a market in that era.

Monmouth is also proud of its association with Lord Nelson which arose from his visit in 1802 when he sailed up the Wye in his admirals barge. He was greatly impressed by the patriotism of the inhabitants and this was probably as a result of his visit to the Naval Temple, erected in full view on the Kymin, the prominent hill across the Wye.

Whether setting out on The Wysis Way from Monmouth, or joining from Offa's Dyke Trail or the Wye Valley Walk, the bridge over the Wye is the start point. From the town an underpass provides safe passage to the riverside. With Offa's Dyke Path, cross the bridge to the east bank and, leaving the river, walk along Gloucester Road for a quarter of a mile passing the May Hill Hotel. In a further 100 yards join a footpath on the right which climbs above the road and follow this to join Kymin Road as far as a sharp right hand bend. Follow Offa's Dyke Path left into Garth Wood and at a junction of paths turn right and follow a well worn path uphill through an open field.

Offa's Dyke Path National Trail was opened in 1971 and follows closely the great earth work built to the order of Offa ,the powerful King of Mercia in the 8th Century. The Trail offers 168 miles of splendid walking along the Welsh border between Chepstow and Prestatyn on the North Wales coast. Offa's Dyke Trail also connects with the Shropshire Way (172 miles) at Clun and Glyndwr's Way (120 miles) at Knighton.

The Wye Valley Walk commences at Chepstow Castle and follows, for 70 miles, the beautiful Wye Valley to Tintern, and then the meandering river past Monmouth, Ross-on Wye and Hereford, to Hay-on-Wye, deep in the Welsh Marches.

From the field join a narrow lane for 20 yards to a sharp right bend and follow a footpath on the left, uphill into Beaulieu Wood, *stepping over outcrops of pudding stone which are a feature of this part of the Forest of Dean.* Emerging at the ridge top The Wysis Way parts from the National Trail and continues straight over a small plateau to a stile.

It is well worth diverting with Offa's Dyke Path for the short distance to the Roundhouse on the summit of The Kymin, where a pause provides opportunity to take in the sweeping view over Monmouth and the Wye valley. The memory of this view may provide a sharp contrast to the Thames side scene later in the journey. A few yards further along the ridge is the Naval Temple, erected by the townspeople in 1800 as a memorial to the Battle of the Nile and to perpetuate the fame of sixteen admirals from an era of British naval glory.

Continuing from the stile, ignore a path following the boundary fence and walk down hill diagonally left, passing a fence corner and through a narrow belt of trees to a gate and stile. Descend a short field, cross a further stile and continue down a track beneath massive oak and beech trees to the Monmouth - Gloucester road. Cross, slightly left, and continue down, now under young oak trees to a forestry road. Follow this to the right to a junction and take the right branch, which soon climbs, curving left.

This part of the Forest is known as High Meadow Woods and although there are many old public roads and footpaths, some of these can be hard to find through new planting or thick undergrowth. Additionally, being subject to forestry operations, the otherwise firm tracks may become badly churned when felling takes place. This is adequately compensated by the many other pleasant paths and tracks available.

Access generally throughout the forest is, more often than not, a pleasant experience, although many of the tracks provided for forestry operations do not coincide with public rights of way or routes shown on maps. A further anomaly is that while Monmouthshire County Council recorded many public paths in the Forest, Gloucestershire claimed none, until more recently, when a few rights of way were agreed with the Forestry Commission.

The Wysis Way follows an old public road well maintained for Forestry use. At the next junction take the track left and follow this for about a mile to the Suck Stone. *This massive detached boulder has been estimated to weigh 12000 tons.*

Climb steeply to the right of the Suck Stone and pass between two detached boulders to reach the limestone outcrop interestingly named Near Hearkening Rock. Climb up left to the top of the cliffs and continue beyond for 100 yards or so to emerge onto a major track. Turn left, ignore a track forking left, and instead, either follow the major track curving right, or, preferably, follow a lesser track on the right from the apex of the curve. At the next path junction keep right *and after a few yards leave Wales and enter England.* Keep left at the next junction and, shortly, fork right down to rejoin the main track recently left. Cross this and descend a path alongside the boundary fence of Lady Park Nature Reserve. As the fence bends left continue downhill over another cross track.

At the valley bottom ignore local waymarking to the left, cross a forestry road, and climb a track uphill to the left. As this track levels out follow a left fork along the contour, curving left and then right and passing a track joining from the left. The path climbs steeply for a few yards to a further junction where The Wysis Way again forks left and descends to a track in the valley bottom. Follow this to the right rising slightly, to a junction. Ignore both of the main tracks and instead turn left onto an indistinct path. Descend, and within a few yards, cross a small stream and then climb steeply up a loose slope and onto a new forestry road. The line of the path has been spoilt when the new road was cut, but cross over and scramble up the embankment. Persevere uphill on an improving path passing a track from the left and continue along the level for a few yards before climbing again .Cross a further track and shortly join a track from the left up to the road at Hillersland. *The Rock Inn, can be found a short distance along the road to the left.*

Turn right, passing an artistic collage built into a garden wall on the left. In 200 yards, pass a telephone kiosk and take the narrow road on the left, which continues as a public footpath. Just prior to reaching the out buildings at Blackthorns Farm, fork left through a gap in the boundary hedge and walk inside the field to a cross hedge and then fork right to rejoin the track, now with the hedge on the left. *After a few yards it is worth pausing to take in the extensive view behind, obscured until now by the tree canopy.*

Continue through two gateways, and then a large open field to a stile onto a lane. Turn right, and after 50 yards, left, onto a headland path and descend a field *with views to the opposite ridge and the village of Christchurch to the right.* At the next boundary follow a footpath diagonally left down the field to Bicknor Street.

Cross to a stile and follow the path down alongside the hedgerow to a gate into a short length of enclosed track. *After passing a barn the path detours around a coppice containing the ruins of a lime kiln.*

Pass through a field gate and walk along a narrow valley to a stile and junction of paths. Turn sharp right crossing another stile and follow the hedgerow uphill. Where this curves right continue up the slope inclining right to a stile in the hedge on the horizon.

Over this turn left and follow the hedgerow down over further stiles and passing close to an old stone barn. Continue up a field, still with the hedge on the left, to a track leading to Lower Carters Piece Farm. A path may be found straight over the track, otherwise, turn right for about 100 yards and then left, doubling back above the farm track. Again after 100 yards, and near a boundary fence, take an indistinct forest path to the right and walk uphill to Carters Piece Picnic Site.

Follow the surfaced road round to the left and cross a turning area to a wide path which continues eastwards through the woods for about 300 yards. Just before reaching a road junction turn right under beech trees and cross the Gloucester - Monmouth Road to a gate and stile, into an area of woodland called *Sallowvallets Inclosure. Sallow Vallets- (salh=willows) (fællet=clump of felled trees).*

Follow the broad path to a T junction and turn right down to a stile in a boundary fence. Cross the track immediately beyond and walk down to a major forestry road and turn left. Where the road commences a sharp curve round to the right, turn off on a path on the right descending into a valley and curving left alongside a stream, the oddly named Rope House Ditch.

THE WYSIS WAY

The reason for this intriguing name is not obvious, particularly as close inspection shows that the stream has been canalised with a concrete bed and sides. There is no evidence that a rope works existed in the locality, and in any event this would probably have resulted in the more commonly named Rope House Walk associated with rope works. Enquiries locally produced an authoritative account from retired local miner Mr. Harvey Gwilliam. He recalls that at the time that many mines and workings in this part of the Forest were closing, improvements were being made to the flow of the stream. Use was made of some of the miles of wire rope, which had suddenly become obsolete, as reinforcing for the concrete used to line the stream.

> *In Devil's Chapel they dug the Ore*
> *A thousand years ago, and more.*
> *Earth's veins of gleaming metal showing*
> *like crusted blood first set aglowing*
> *Phoenician faces.*
>
> F W Harvey

Follow the path and stream down to a wide junction and turn onto a track to the right. After approximately 500 yards a less prominent track makes a hairpin turn back to the left. Follow this down to cross the Rope House Ditch again and another hairpin turn back to the right before continuing eastwards. Cross a forestry track and continue, still following the stream, over a junction, with two paths on the left and a single path to the right.

Very shortly cross a tributary of the Cannop Brook, which Rope House Ditch joins, and walk up to the Parkend - Lydbrook road. Turn right for a few paces and then left on a track leading to a car park and picnic area on the site of the *Old Speculation Mine*. From the parking area walk uphill to a cycle track along the bed of the old railway line. Walk left to a signpost where the cycle route diverges from the line of the railway. Turn right from the signpost on a path angling up the slope. Towards the top join a path from the left and walk up to the ridge. Turn left on the broad uphill path, but after 100 yards fork right on a path along the contour. At the boundary wall of Serridge Lodge join a track and follow this left up to rejoin the main ridge track.

The industrialisation of Dean in the 18th Century was retarded by the poor condition of roads in the area. In winter these were largely impassable and at best required large teams of horses to move wagons of ore and coal. This led, around 1800, to the building of horse tram roads linking many mines throughout the forest to the Severn, at Lydney and Bullo Pill, and to the Wye, at Monmouth.

The tramways consisted of a track bed on which were laid L section iron plates, at first only three feet long, on which the flangeless wagon wheels ran. The rails were notched at the joints and "nails" were driven into oak plugs set in square stone sleepers. The 3'6" gauge was later converted to Broad gauge and later tram roads were Standard gauge "edge" railways. From 1840 many tramways changed to steam working alongside the railways being extended through the forest. Little trace now remains of a complex network apart from the track beds which make such good walking and cycle tracks today.

Walk along the ridge for about 350 yards, passing a tree covered spoil tip to a stile on the right.

Descend close to the steep side of the tip and continue down to a stile leading to the site of *Trafalgar Colliery and railway siding*. Turn right to a track and follow this left passing Trafalgar House where drinks and snacks are usually available.

The 'gale', or licence to mine Trafalgar was granted to Cornelius Brain of Mitcheldean in 1842, although work there did not begin until 1860. Trafalgar Colliery was unique in being gas lit, which was only possible because the Forest of Dean coalfield was completely free of firedamp (methane). Brain and his brothers already worked the colourfully named mines, the 'Strip and at It' and 'Rose in Hand'.

One brother, Frank, had been associated with the use of electric floodlights on the Severn Railway Bridge in 1879, where they had been used to enable work to be carried on at night to make best use of the tides. The powerful lamps were later erected at Trafalgar to light the colliery yard. The installation of electric pumping at Trafalgar in 1882, was the first such recorded use in mines.

The track, gently descending for half a mile, is the line of *'Brains tramway'* in use by the colliery before the railway was extended from Cinderford. It eventually emerges from the trees alongside the boundary of the long dismantled railway. Continue for 100 yards crossing a major forestry road, into an enclosed green track, *where the route is now shared with the Gloucestershire Way for about 3 miles to Plump Hill. Over the fence on the right, Drybrook Road Station once stood.*

The Gloucestershire Way is a continuous path of 100 miles from Chepstow to Tewkesbury, and passing through Gloucester and Stow on the Wold. The route was conceived on a theme of 'Forest and Vale and High Blue Hill' from a poem 'A song of Gloucestershire' by F W Harvey.

The Gloucestershire Way also provides a through link between Offa's Dyke Trail and the Oxfordshire Way, Heart of England Way and Worcestershire Way.

Continue along this track for about 500 yards until it converges with the bed of the old railway again. Keep left for a few yards and then turn left uphill and shortly cross a forest track and an area recently felled and replanted. Cross a further track and walk uphill on a pleasant path beneath conifers. At an obvious left bend continue on a fainter path directly uphill to a stile and then under young larch trees to a second stile.

Continue over another track uphill, at first under sweet chestnut and then beech trees crowning the summit of the ridge.

Descend the far side keeping to the line of a sunken pathway to reach a triangle of forest roads. Either cross directly or follow the angle of one of the roads to an open space adjacent to factory buildings. A stile and gate on the right lead into Hawkwell Inclosure and a path beneath mature oak trees. Cross a small stream and then a stile in a fence, *with Cinderford coming into view on the hills to the right*. Continue along a track under tall conifers to a second stile, and an area recently underplanted after felling, follow the track left at a fork to a final stile before reaching a road at Nailbridge.

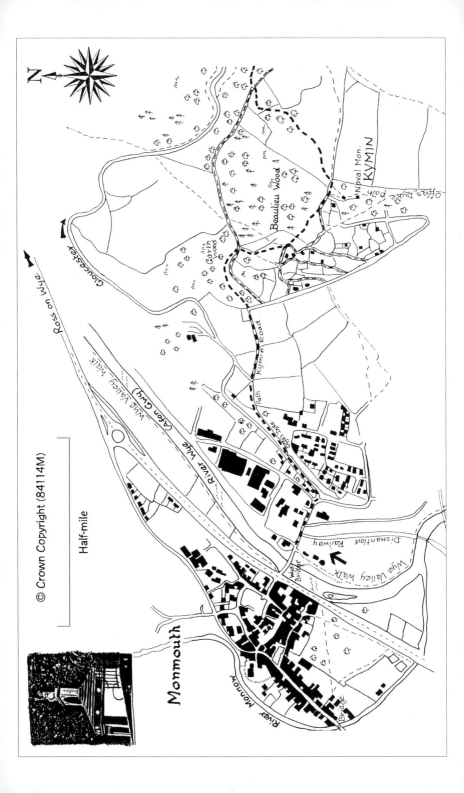

© Crown Copyright (8114M)

Half-mile

N

Ross on Wye

Gloucester

Monmouth

River Wye (Afon Gwy)

Wye Valley Walk

River Wye

River Monnow

Bridge

Wye Bridge

Wye Valley Walk

Dismantled Railway

Dixe's Dyke

Path

Kymin Road

Garth Wood

Beaulieu Wood

Naval Mon.

KYMIN

Offa's Dyke Path

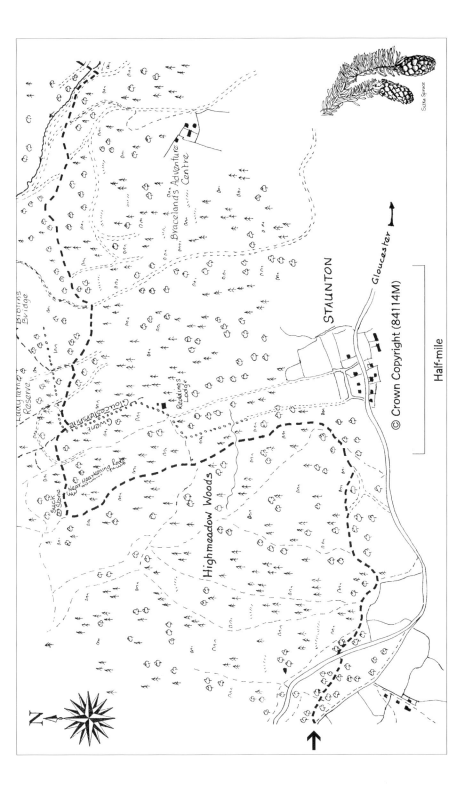

Highmeadow Woods

STAUNTON

Gloucester →

Bracelands Adventure Centre

Biblins Bridge

Highbury Reserve

Gwent / Gloucestershire

Reddings Lodge

Suck Stone

Near Hearkening Rocks

N

© Crown Copyright (84114M)

Half-mile

Sitka Spruce

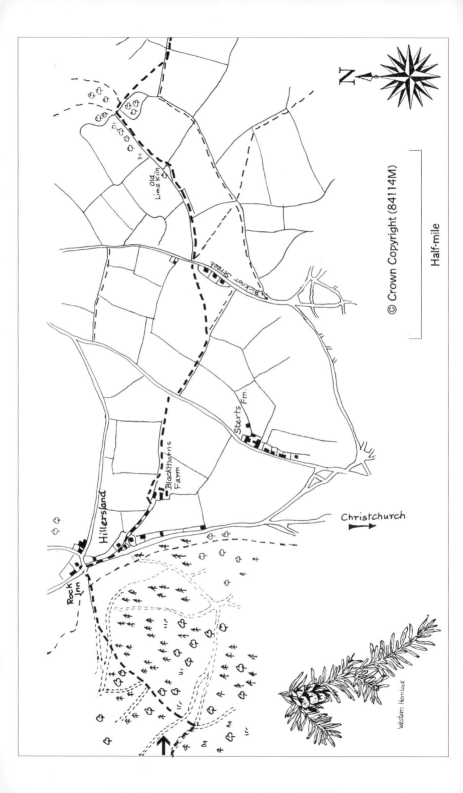

N

© Crown Copyright (84114M)

Half-mile

Old Lime Kiln

Bicknor Street

Sterts Fm.

Blackthorns Farm

Hillersland

Rock Inn

Christchurch

Western Hemlock

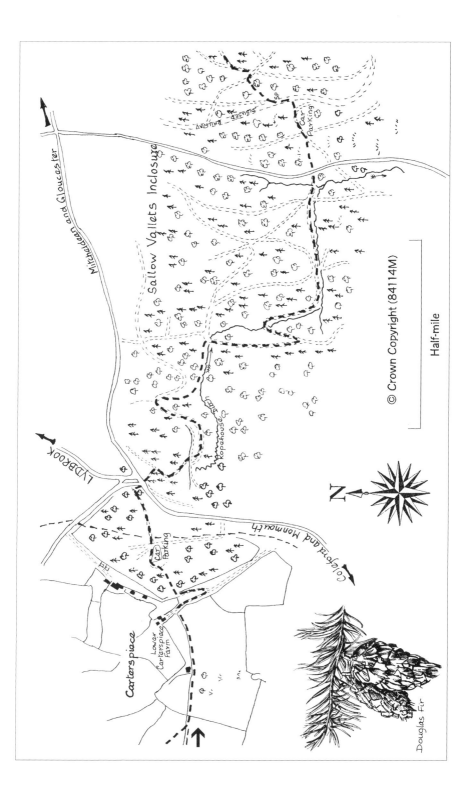

Mitcheldean and Gloucester

LYDBROOK

Coleford and Monmouth

Carterspiece

Lower
Carterspiece
Farm

Car Parking

Sallow Vallets Inclosure

Kidnalls

DISUSED RAILWAY

Car Parking

SP

© Crown Copyright (84114M)

Half-mile

N

Douglas Fir

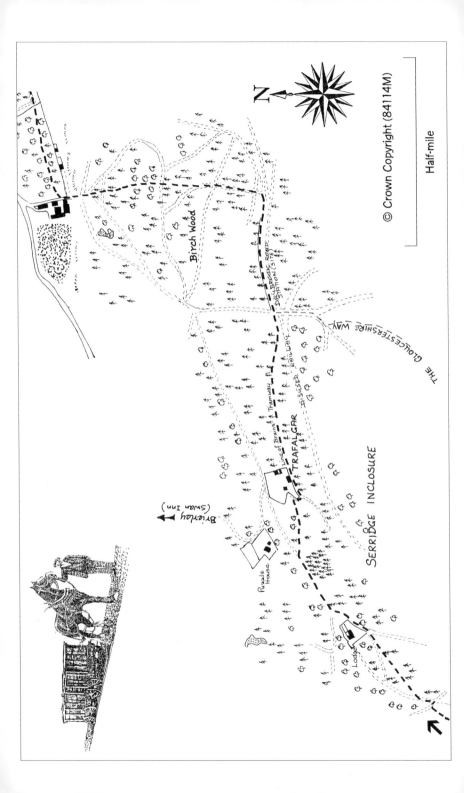

N

© Crown Copyright (84114M)

Half-mile

Birch Wood

Dilbrook Gorse
STATION (STE

THE GLOUCESTERSHIRE WAY

Line of Brain's Tramway

DISUSED RAILWAY

TRAFALGAR

SERRIDGE INCLOSURE

Birtway
(Swan Inn)

Puzzle House

Lodge

Nailbridge - Barbers Bridge

Cross to a footpath alongside a house and then over open ground to join a lane near a wayside stone, probably an old gatepost. Cross a stream to a stile alongside a gate, turn left and walk behind cottages to a second stile giving entry to a lawn and garden. The public path angles to the right to pass between the buttresses of an old railway bridge and continues under an avenue of fine oak trees until a white house comes into view. Then follow the boundary wall to a cross track with a vehicle barrier and a massive oak tree on the right.

Cross the track and turn half left under further oak trees, and walk up to the Gloucester-Monmouth road. Turn right and cross the road onto a forest track and take the right fork within a few paces. Walk uphill to join another track from the left and at the next fork take the left branch to the top of the slope. Cross another track and walk downhill on a pleasant path edged with beech trees. Cross an old tramway and continue down a path sometimes overgrown by gorse and bracken to a stile. Through *the trees on the right is Merring Meend, a hilltop lake and an attractive spot for rest and refreshment.*

Emerge into a parking area and turn right to a small crossroads, where the Gloucestershire Way continues downhill. Instead, take the lane to the left, signposted to The Wilderness Field Study Centre, and walk up for 300 yards to pass two bungalows on the right.

Alternative Route (avoiding Mitcheldean)

Ignore a footpath signposted left, and turn right to follow a track curving left behind a house boundary. At a junction with a lane, bear left and follow the lane which curves right and up to a boundary fence of a garden. Follow the track uphill alongside the garden and, after passing the entrance to 'Four Winds', turn left on a track towards a field. Before reaching a gate, fork right on a grassy track which slants down the contours to the Gloucester-Monmouth road.

Cross over to a footpath alongside a barn and follow a fence down to a stile onto a narrow lane. Turn left for 100 yards to a stile on the right and walk uphill towards a lone oak tree. Pass this, and gradually converge with a school boundary fence to reach a kissing gate onto Abenhall Lane. Turn right and cross the road to a bridleway track and after 50 yards turn left through a gate. Cross the field to a further gate and walk up the next field, with the hedge on the left. *From this slight elevation there is a skyline-view of May Hill summit in front with Breakheart Hill to the left. Over your shoulder is Plump Hill, the Wilderness, and to the north Wigpool Common, overlooking Worcestershire.*

A stile descends into woodland and a path, sometimes hidden by undergrowth, angles slightly left, steeply down to a further stile. Over this, turn diagonally right, cross a fence and walk down to a stile and steps descending the verge of Gloucester-Monmouth road, near Abenhall Mill.

Turn right for about 300 yards to a footpath on the left passing through a pedestrian gate at 'Harts Barn', a craft and flower shop with a handy tea room. Cross a gravelled area and climb steps to a stile, turn right and follow a fence uphill to a gate. Through this, ignore a track descending from the left and cross to a further gate, then follow a headland track uphill. At a further gate, cross a culvert over a deep gulley and walk on the level to the middle of the next field. About 100 yards below an isolated oak tree angle downhill to the right to a gate in the hedge corner. Through this turn immediately right through a further gate and then climb the field angling left about 45 degrees to a gate in a hedge. Cross a further field directly to a gate and descend the next field, again about 45 degrees left, to a stile in the corner into woodland. Follow an enclosed track down, shortly passing along the edge of a cottage garden, and descend to join a bridleway. Turn right, climbing to a brow and then walk down, for about 100 yards, to a footpath up steps on the left.

Climb the steps on a path again shared with the Gloucestershire Way. Walk down the field diagonally left to a stile, found down to the right, just before reaching a stone boundary wall in front. Turn left along the village street to the junction with the Gloucester-Ross road and follow the pavement to the Nags Head Inn.

Possibly refreshed, cross the road to a footpath through the car park and descend the field to a footbridge over a stream. Beyond, cross the embankment of the old railway and then angle left to a stile and descend the steep verge to a road and rejoin the Wysis Way coming from Mitcheldean.

After the second bungalow, turn left onto a footpath along the edge of woodland passing under occasional beech trees, aptly named 'Beech Walk'. Over a slight brow, where the path begins to descend left, turn right through a kissing gate and cross a field on a line towards the summit of May Hill on the horizon. *The slight elevation of this field gives splendid views behind, from Ruardean and Drybrook around to the Malverns, deep in Worcestershire.*

Cross a stile and follow a boundary wall down to a further stile. The path curves left alongside an old hedgerow, and descends to a kissing gate. *The extensive views are now to the east over the Severn Vale. Robinswood Hill, prominent above Gloucester, and Painswick Beacon high on the scarp beyond, give the route of The Wysis Way across Cotswold. To the right, in the vale, is the serpentine course of the Severn.*

Continue down, *with a panorama of Mitcheldean below, dominated by the sprawl of the Rank Xerox works*. At a final stile from the hillside turn right and follow the narrow street down to a junction with May Meadow Lane. Turn left and cross a road, lined on one side with a row of medieval shopfronts, to the 14 Century parish church of St. Michael and All Angels. Follow the churchyard path, through an avenue of sculpted yews, to the High Street and follow this left for a short distance to Townend and then continue down Bradley Court Road.

Continue past the extensive buildings of Rank Xerox for about half a mile, ignoring a footpath on the right, to a second path, alongside a cottage. Walk up a headland track and at the first gateway, either continue following the headland to Bilbut Farm, or better, go left and angle up the adjacent field to a lane. *It is well worth pausing for the view behind of Wigpool Common with the Wilderness and Plump Hill away to the left.*

Continue up the lane, past farm buildings, to the ridgetop, and descend the short length of enclosed lane curving right to a gate, where the bridleway continues alongside the hedge. The Wysis Way descends straight down the contours to a stile in a wire fence. Cross a field to further stile and walk alongside a hedge, consisting mainly of elm and holly trees, up to a gate and stile, *framing May Hill summit beyond.*

From the gate, follow a wire fence up to a further gate. Cross the stile on the left into the adjacent field and follow the headland now with the hedge on the right. Through a gate continue along the boundary hedge of the next field to a stile in the corner. Descend the field, close to three oak trees to a stile set under ash trees. Then walk steeply down an open field, *where the hedges, which may still be shown on OS maps, no longer exist*, to the left of a white cottage. A stile in the corner, hidden from view until the last moment, exits onto the Gloucester-Ross road. *The Farmers Boy Inn is about 100 yards to the left, while the Nags Head Inn is about 300 yards to the right. Either way, be careful of the traffic approaching around the bends.*

Turn right, and in a few yards, left, down a lane. Cross a stream and walk up to rejoin the alternative route and the Gloucestershire Way. Turn right into a narrow lane signed 'No Through Road' and walk steeply up to a bend at Mutlow. Immediately after the second cottage turn right and climb steep steps and a stile.

A pleasant path curves up the hillside to a coppice with a stile, slightly right, hidden under the overhanging trees. Through the coppice, continue uphill alongside a hedge and over further stiles, to reach Yartleton Lane. Turn left for 20 yards, and then right, up a narrow track through National Trust land to the summit of May Hill. The acre or so containing the tree clad summit is owned by the parish of Longhope *'for the rest and recreation of the parishioners!'*

There are said to be 99 trees in the summit clump and superstition is that a 100th tree will not grow. As the Celts are said to have worshipped Baal here, and the Romans their goddess Maia, it is not surprising that old superstitions still linger.

From the summit of May Hill survey the dark wooded ridge of Dean and the whole of the rich red vale of the River Leadon. Looking north, over Newent, is Dymock where the 'Dymock poets' wrote themselves into fame during their brief stay in the locality immediately before the first World War.

THE WYSIS WAY

From Marcle way,
From Dymock, Kempley, Newent, Bromsberrow,
Redmarley, all the meadowland daffodils seem
Running in golden tides to Ryton firs,
To make the knot of steep little wooded hills
There brightest show: O bella eth de loro!

Lascelles Abercrombie

Although the 'muse colony' as they came to be known; Lascelles
Abercrombie, Wilfred Gibson and Robert Frost; were not
Gloucestershire poets, they received many visitors during their stay
who were also destined to become well known. Of these, Rupert
Brooke, perhaps the most well known, and Edward Thomas, were
shortly to die in war. Among the local poets who visited the colony,
John Drinkwater later lived at Far Oakridge, and W.H. Davies at
Nailsworth. John Haines, a Gloucester solicitor, was a regular visitor
and particular friend of Robert Frost. Although he wrote little poetry
himself, Haines greatly encouraged Ivor Gurney and F.W. (Will)
Harvey who were later to become acknowledged poets, and Harvey
Laureate of Gloucestershire.

From the summit of May Hill turn right, and descend, with the
Gloucestershire Way, towards the southeast. Through a gate, at the
boundary of the National Trust land, walk down an enclosed track to a
pole barrier. Continue over a crosstrack and at a fork turn left, *leaving*
the Gloucestershire Way, down a green lane, passing close to an *'art*
deco' house with an indoor pool set in Victorian tiles and pillars.

At a junction of tracks below the house, turn left over a stile and shortly
fork right. Descend pleasantly through woodland consisting of sweet
chestnut, sycamore, holly, oak, beech, and larch, *with glimpses of the*
Severn Vale and the Cotswold scarp through the trees.

NAILBRIDGE - BARBERS BRIDGE

At a further junction, bear right, still descending, now under a canopy of fir trees, to a road at Glasshouse. Turn right, passing a Victorian postbox and then a cottage with a fine topiarian reflection of itself.

At the beginning of the 17 Century, industry was widespread throughout the countryside although, apart from concentrated localities, such as the Forest of Dean, the visible signs were not obvious. In many areas where timber was available for making charcoal small scale glass making occurred. Later refining processes were improved by the addition of ash from burnt bracken.

Cross the road to a footpath passing behind the Glasshouse Inn, *probably too early after the Farmers Boy to seek further refreshment.* After 150 yards the wide track narrows at a junction, take the left fork past a cottage, and after a further 40 yards, turn left onto a path twisting through coppiced woodland alongside a stream.

Cross a gully, with a stream flowing into that on the left, and walk up to a track. The definitive line of the path has been obstructed by the creation of a lake but this has resulted in an attractive alternative route which is likely to become the legal path in the near future. Follow the track left, for no more than 40 yards, then turn left to a path at the edge of the lake in a pleasing woodland setting.

At the end of the lake turn left along the grass dam to about the mid-point, then slant down right, to regain the original line of the path alongside the stream. This pleasant woodland path ends all too soon at a stile into open fields. Cross two stiles in quick succession over a track which leads up to an attractive red brick farmhouse on the left. Continue up the middle of a meadow to a gate and stile onto a lane. Cross over to a farm drive and walk up to Byfords farm, where the path bears left past the farm outbuildings. Pass through a gate and cross a small paddock to a further gate, and walk down the next field close to the stream on the left, to a stile and footbridge hidden in the corner.

Walk through two small fields to a lake set below the extensive farm buildings of Hownhall and cross a concrete farm bridge. Turn right within a few yards along a meadow to a gate in the far hedge. The correct line is about midway between the stream on the right and trees indicating an old field boundary on the left.

At the gate turn left on Moat Lane and walk up towards the outskirts of Taynton. At a junction turn right, past cottages, but leave the track almost immediately, turning left along a headland path with a hedge to the left. Through a gateway continue to the next field boundary and a crossroad of footpaths in a small hollow beneath an oak tree.

Continue along the headland to the next boundary and then turn half right up the field beyond. *The slight elevation of this field gives splendid views around the horizon.* Angle down the slight slope towards the far corner of this long field, to a metal gate which is about fifty yards left of the actual corner. From the gate walk under two oak trees and cross a farm drive, with further oak trees away to the left, to a footbridge.

Cross the bridge, and ignoring a path straight on, curve left, to a ditch crossing with double stiles. Cross the next long field, in line with two white houses prominent in the distance, to a stile slightly left of two oak trees in the hedge. *Tibberton Court is on the high ground to the right shielded by trees.* From the stile cross the field diagonally to converge with the hedge on the left.

Through a gap in the corner of the field boundary follow a track uphill past a small coppice. *While climbing the slope, pause to look back to May Hill prominent in the west, to the north, Ragged Stone Hill stands at the end of the Malvern ridge.*

NAILBRIDGE - BARBERS BRIDGE

Near Bullenbank, on Gloucester road,
Thy everlasting mercy showed
The ploughman patient on the hill
For ever there, for ever still,
Ploughing the hill with steady yoke
Of pine-trees lightning-struck and broke.
I've marked the May Hill ploughman stay
There on his hill, day after day
Driving his team against the sky

John Masefield

The track joins a road at Tibberton where the attractive thirteenth century church, just to the right provides a pleasant spot to stop for refreshment.

Turn left on the road down to a junction and then right, passing the village pond. Within a few yards, turn left along Orchard Rise and take care not to overlook the second of two footpaths between the houses on the left hand side. Walk behind the houses to reach a footbridge leading into an open field and cross to converge with the hedge on the right, and walk around a corner to a hidden gate.

Walk diagonally left up the next field on a line left of farm buildings, and continue through the farmyard. Walk down a short paddock to a gate and follow a headland track towards a small coppice of fir trees, the site of the old Railway Station. At a road turn left, over Barbers Bridge and the dismantled railway, and then immediately right, down the embankment to the modern road bypassing the bridge.

31

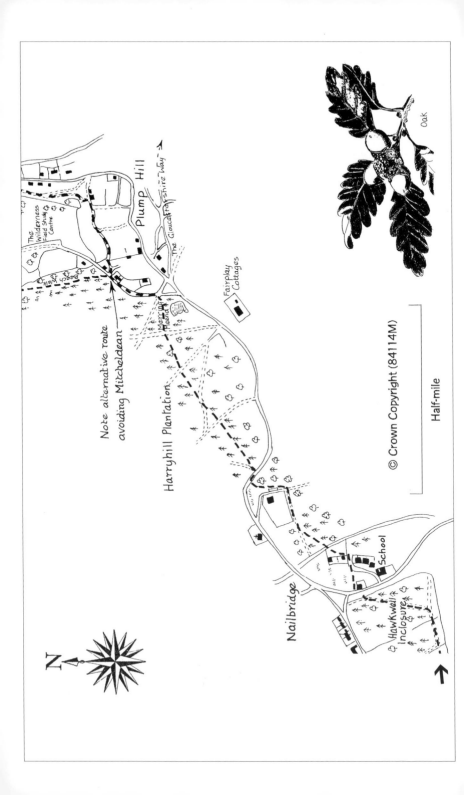

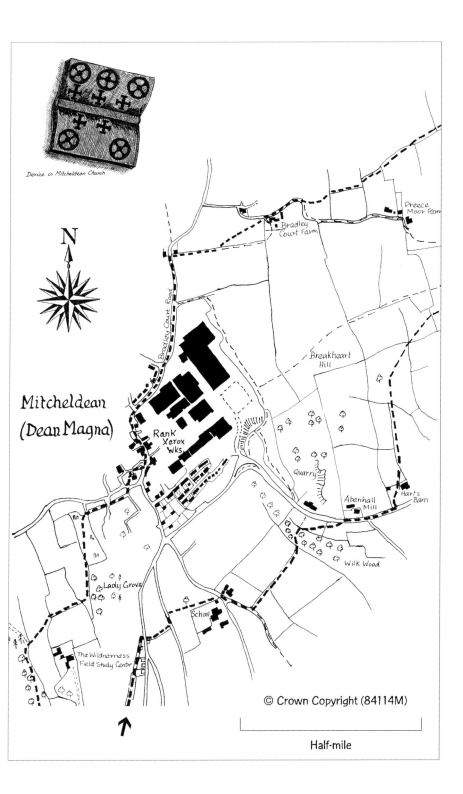

Device in Mitcheldean Church

N

Mitcheldean
(Dean Magna)

Bradley Court Road

Bradley
Court Farm

Preece
Moor Farm

Breakheart
Hill

Rank
Xerox
Wks.

Quarry

Abenhall
Mill

Harts
Barn

Wilk Wood

Lady Grove

School

The Wildnerness
Field Study Centre

© Crown Copyright (84114M)

Half-mile

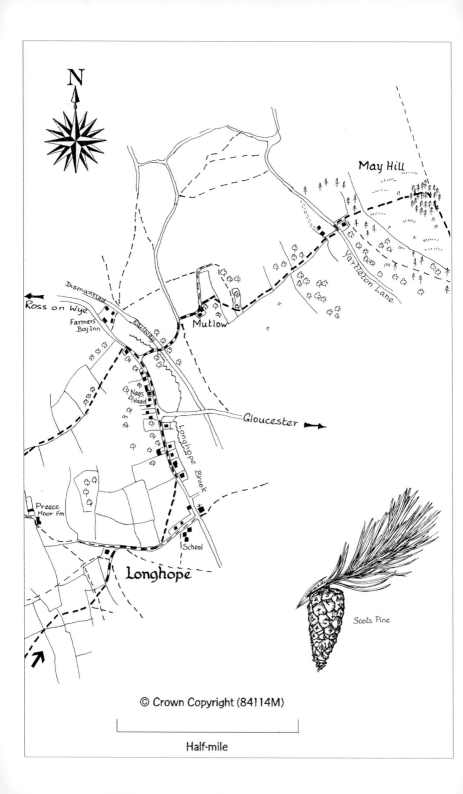

N

May Hill

Ross on Wye

Dismantled

Farmers
Boy Inn

Railway

Mutlow

Yartleton Lane

Gloucester ►

Nags
Head

Longhope Brook

Preece
Moor Fm

School

Longhope

Scots Pine

© Crown Copyright (84114M)

Half-mile

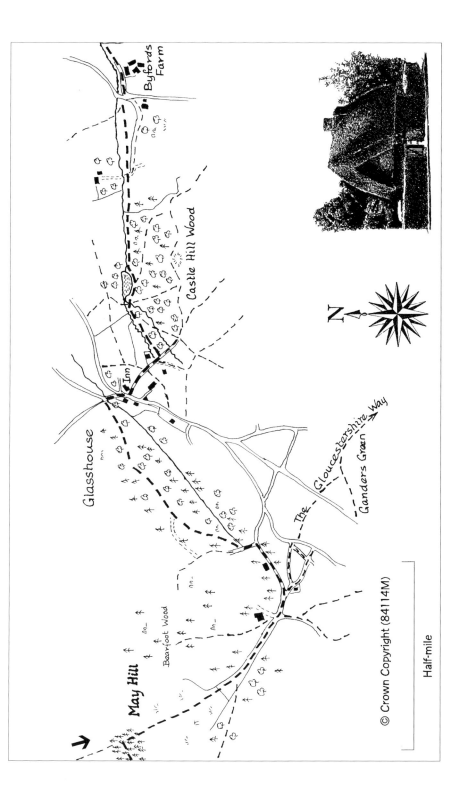

May Hill

Glasshouse

Bear-foot Wood

Castle Hill Wood

Inn

Byfords Farm

The Gloucestershire Way

Ganders Green

N

© Crown Copyright (84114M)

Half-mile

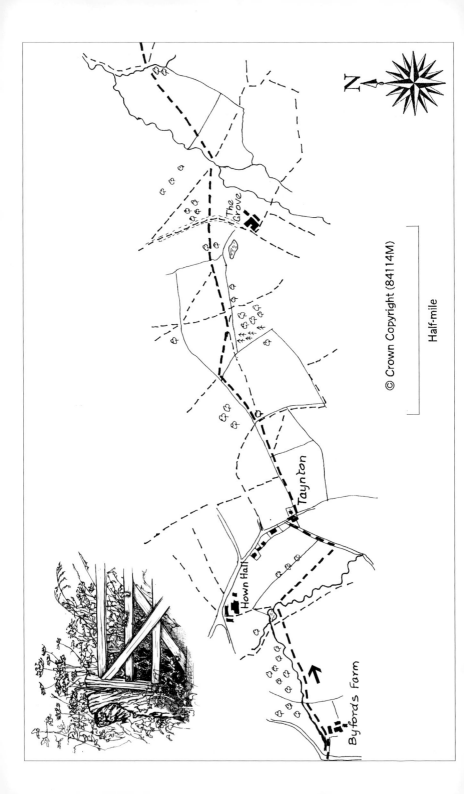

N

The Grove

Taynton

Hown Hall

Byfords Farm

© Crown Copyright (84114M)

Half-mile

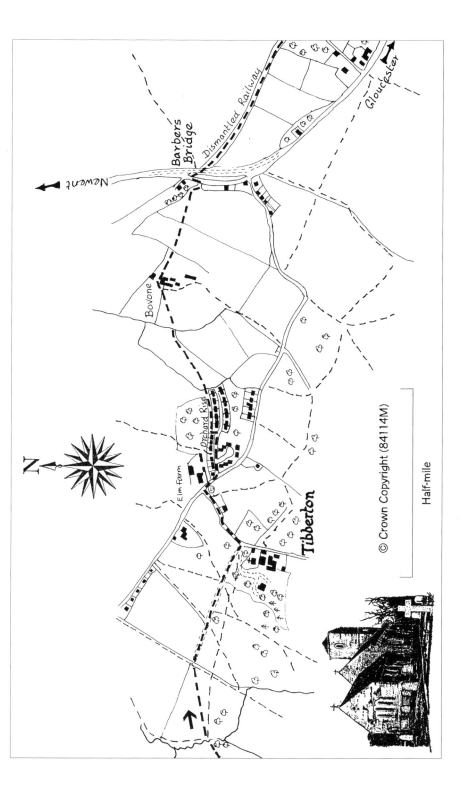

N

Newent

Barbers
Bridge

Dismantled Railway

Gloucester

Bovone

Orchard Rise

Elm Farm

Tibberton

© Crown Copyright (8411AM)

Half-mile

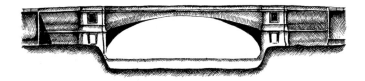

Barbers Bridge - Painswick Beacon

Turn right along the verge for a few yards before crossing to a stile and follow a footpath along the bed of the old railway for about three quarters of a mile. At Rudford Church the footpath leaves the railway cutting climbing up right to the road bridge.

Cross the road to a stile and follow the hedge. At the next boundary, the path has been diverted to follow the hedgerow to a further stile on the left. Over this continue along the bed of the railway to a stile in a fence. Cross this and immediately turn right through a gate into a field. Do not follow the path to a road, but instead turn left along a bridleway, which commences from the road, and follow this, alongside the shallow depression of an old canal, curving left to a hunt gate into woodland.

> *The Herefordshire and Gloucestershire canal was commenced in 1792 but did not reach Hereford until 1845, too late to be viable. The canal was 34 miles in length, from the River Severn at Gloucester via Newent, Dymock and Ledbury, with 22 locks and three tunnels. The canal closed in 1881 to allow the construction of the Gloucester to Newent railway and the track was laid along some lengths of the canal bed.*

Through the gate, the bridleway soon climbs gradually to follow the edge of the wood before turning right on a good track and crossing a field for 100 yards or so. Follow the track left through farm buildings to a lane near a disused church tower. *Originally Saxon, Lassington Church was dedicated on Palm Sunday, 1095 AD.*

Turn right and follow the lane around a bend to a footpath through a gate on the left. Walk to a second gate with a stile alongside. Cross this, and then a second stile immediately on the right, into a narrow paddock, at the far end of which a stile leads into a grass and woodland area at Maidenhall. Follow a path uphill to the left to a stile and cross a field diagonally right, to a further stile.

Gloucester and the cathedral are visible past the edge of the woodland in front and beyond is the sweep of the Cotswold scarp. To the north is the high ground of Cleeve Hill and the outlying Oxenton and Alderton Hills. Above Wainloads Hill in the foreground is the long low bulk of Bredon Hill. Further left, over your shoulder, and the vale of the Leadon, lie the Malvern Hills.

Who says 'Gloucester' sees a tall
Fair fashioned shape of stone arise,
That changes with the changing skies
From joy to funeral gloom,
Then quick again to joy;
...
Far Cotswolds all a- shimmer,
Blue Bredon leagues away—
Huge Malverns, farther, dimmer...

Ivor Gurney

Over the stile, turn left to a second stile into Lassington Wood. There are several routes through the woodland, not all public rights of way. A pleasant path descends left and along the bottom of the wood. At a junction with a path from the right continue down to a stile at the wood end. Over this incline left to an enclosed track, Lassington Lane. The *pinnacles of Gloucester cathedral glimpsed over the trees.*

Follow the lane for over half a mile to the Gloucester-Ross road at Over. Turn left, *perhaps pausing at the Dog Inn*, before crossing the dual carriageway to Over Bridge spanning the west channel of the Severn. The bridge, an English Heritage site, is pleasantly isolated from the nearby rush of traffic, and provides the start of a quiet route into the city.

Designed by Thomas Telford and copied from a bridge over the Seine it was opened in 1831. The arch is a graceful ellipse enhanced by the chamfering of the stonework to ease the flow of floodwaters. A keen eye will detect where the crown of the arch sank considerably when the scaffolding was first removed. No doubt a heart stopping moment for the site engineers, but Telford's letter to the City fathers explains that this is not a problem! The bridge replaced a 13th century structure of eight arches.

Although no longer carrying the road, the bridge is quite properly a protected structure, and provides passage for both the Wysis Way and the Gloucestershire Way, over the western channel of the Severn. Modern road construction has removed much of the medieval causeway between Telford's bridge and the city, and a direct route no longer exists.

During the winter months the River Severn is liable to overflow the low-lying areas between the two channels of the river. The only option then is to continue alongside the road from the Dog Inn into the city. For most of the year however, several routes are available without using roads.

Alternative Route

From the bridge walk down the grass slope and cross to a footbridge over a stream, turn right and walk under the causeway alongside the mainline railway. The *cathedral tower, framed by the concrete piers, creates a powerful image of ancient and modern.*

At the next stile turn right along the boundary of a sports field, *Gloucester Irish Associations Hurling Pitch*. Reaching the railway viaduct, turn right through an arch to a gate and follow a track to reach the road and turn left to Westgate Bridge. An underpass beneath the carriageway leads to a pedestrian bridge over the east channel of the Severn. Both the Severn Way and the Gloucestershire Way continue north along the east bank of the river.

Opened in 1989, the Severn Way in Gloucestershire runs for 50 miles, along the east bank from Tewkesbury to Sheperdine, just south of Berkeley. Following roads, footpaths and bridleways, often along the floodbank, the route passes through ancient communities and scenes. During the walk the river changes from tree bordered tranquillity at Tewkesbury, to a mile wide tidal estuary at Sheperdine.

A further 220 miles of path has been identified, along or near the river, continuing through Worcestershire and Shropshire. The final section in Powys, through Newtown, Welshpool and Llandiloes will shortly be completed to reach the source of the Severn on Plynlimon.

Walk down the grass slope from the bridge and turn right, under the railway viaduct, to follow both arms of the Severn around the wide expanse of the Port Ham and the Oxleaze. Near Castlemeads car park, a footbridge over the east channel leads directly into the heart of the docks and the city.

THE WYSIS WAY

Rising in the mountains of mid Wales, close to the source of the Wye, the Severn is Britain's longest river.

Although never as important as the Thames, the Severn was, nonetheless, a crucial trade route for centuries. In 1701 there was a regular water taxi between Shrewsbury and Gloucester, and , by the middle of the 18th Century, 100,000 tons of coal was shipped down the river from Coalport annually. Severn Trows of up to 80 tons laden, plied both up and downstream to adjacent Midland towns, the Bristol Channel ports, and beyond. Although a good deal of bow hauling, both by men and horses, was involved, because of the strong tides and fresh water flow, Severn traffic relied far less on towing than Thames craft were obliged to.

The Vale of Severn extends for more than thirty miles, bounded by the Cotswold scarp to the east, and the high ground of Dean to the west. To the north, Tewkesbury stands at the gateway to the Worcestershire plain and the Vale of Evesham. Viewed from Bredon Hill, Gloucester and the cathedral stand boldly in the centre of the vale. To the south the ever widening estuary dominates the Severn Vale.

Until the building of the Severn bridges, Gloucester was, for centuries, the major crossing point of the Severn, an ancient frontier and centre for trade. The Romans early established a fort and Glevum became a place of retirement for officers and administrators. Wherever a hole is dug in the city it is said that 2000 years of occupation will be found.

Following the Romans and Saxons, the Normans commenced work on the cathedral, the tower, 225 feet high, is a landmark for many miles, clearly seen from many points on Cotswold and from Bredon and the Malvern Hills.

BARBERS BRIDGE - PAINSWICK BEACON

In 1089 William the Conqueror gave instructions for the preparation of Domesday Book from his parliament in Gloucester.

Edward II, murdered at nearby Berkeley, was entombed in the cathedral, which, as a result, became a mecca for pilgrims. The prosperity which followed provided the 3000 inhabitants with a total of five monasteries and twelve churches, which in time gave rise to Shakespeare's comment 'as sure as Gods' in Gloucester'.

Unfortunately, the city elders backed Cromwell in the Civil War withstanding a determined and expensive siege by the Kings forces in 1643. On his restoration the King sought his dues and caused the city walls, which would have been the equal of York or Chester today, to be demolished.

Gloucester was granted a charter as a port by Elizabeth I in 1580, complete with its own Customs house. However, Bristol merchants mounted such a furious lobby that the charter was revoked within two years, and it was not until the completion of the Gloucester-Sharpness canal, three centuries later, that Gloucester regained its status as a port.

The area of the docks has been largely restored to present an historic image of the importance of water-borne trade from the Victorian era. The splendid and extensive warehousing and several old sailing vessels, usually moored there, maintain the link with the cities trading history. Although now a popular marina and tourist centre, commercial motor barges, up to 400 tons, still ply the canal to Sharpness, and the river north to Tewkesbury and Worcester.

From the docks area leave by the access at either Llanthony Road or Southgate Street, to the traffic lights at the junction. Walk along Spa Road and across the park, towards Robinswood Hill in the background, to Parkend Road. Turn right to traffic lights at Stroud Road and then follow this left.

The winding course of this tree lined route out of the city softens the impact of walking alongside this busy road and after the tedious crossing of the ring road at St. Barnabas' roundabout, the rush of traffic is thankfully left behind.

Turn left off the roundabout, into the comparative calm of Reservoir Road and follow this for a quarter of a mile and around a sharp bend, to the entrance to Robinswood Hill Country Park. From the entrance gate in Reservoir Road, either follow the roadway, or walk directly up the steep grass slope to the Park buildings. *It is barely two miles from the Docks but most walkers will consider it a great relief to resume walking the Wysis Way in countryside. Although I personally feel some regret that the wild and tangled old hill, with few hidden paths, which I used to walk, has now been tamed as a Country Park.*

Called Robin's Wood in 1777, and Robinhoodes and Mattesknoll in 1799. The name may recall a family Robins, who were tenants of the manor of Matsone in 1526. They also had the lease of Mattesknoll - 'top of knoll'. There is a reference in 1559 to 'a bekn on Matsons Hyll'.

The maze of paths over and around the hill can be confusing, many not being public rights of way or shown on OS maps. The object is to reach the trig point and the most direct path passes behind the Park buildings, slightly left, and then climbs directly to the summit.

From the trig point turn right, south-west, along the ridge for 100 yards to a small col and a cross path. Turn left, downhill, and fork right within a few yards, descending through scrub and then a narrow tree belt, mainly of birch and larch, to a stile. Continue down through more scrub, to the right of a line of poplars, to a track. Follow this to the right and after about 400 yards, locate a stile on the left. Over this, walk steeply down the field towards the thick hedge on the left. Very shortly cross a stile through the hedge, and then skirt the lower edge of a golf course. Follow the hedge, turning right, and after passing a pond and willow trees, cross a culvert over a deep ditch.

Continue with the hedge on your right, *now sharing the path with the Glevum Way, a route circling the city.* Pass a stile where a path joins from the right and continue following the hedge left. Ignore a field gate, but after 300 yards or so, as the hedge bends right, cross a stile and follow a path twisting through undergrowth, to emerge on a lane near a cottage. Follow the lane for about 100 yards, to a gate and turn right along the edge of Sneedhams Green, an old common. At a road turn right and cross over the M5 motorway. Immediately after the bridge, turn left to a stile.

Sneedhams Green, also Snedham and Sneadham, - 'homestead or meadow on a detached piece of land, possibly isolated from a main settlement'.

Cross a field to a stile in a barbed wire fence, and continue on the same line towards a small red brick building on the hillside, to a stile hidden from sight as you approach. Cross this and follow a path uphill to the left of the small building. The path bends right and then left. Ignore a farm track and take a path over a stile on the left, climbing steeply uphill through coppiced hazel and beneath mature oak trees. Leave the wood by a stile and walk along a headland towards houses. Do not pass through a gateway immediately ahead, instead turn right before the houses, on a track leading up to a gate and into a small paddock.

Marked 'traces of paving' on old maps, the footpath is the line of an ancient road called Sandford (sarnfordd: paved way). Traces of slabs could be seen until recently, believed to be Roman from the second century.

Follow the boundary hedge and leave the paddock through a gate, still with the hedge to the right. Veering away from the hedge walk uphill, towards a steep tump, similar to a tumulus, up on the left. Past this continue uphill close to a field boundary on the left until reaching a cross hedge. In the absence of a stile or a way through, follow the hedge right for about 100 yards and go through a gateway. Turn right and walk up an improving track to a gate and turn left onto a narrow lane.

On the right hand verge is King Charles' Stone, where he is said to have surveyed the city during his attempt to lift the siege during the Civil War. More likely to be a boundary marker between the parishes of Painswick and Upton St. Leonard's, it may have been a mounting block for riders having paused to rest after the climb from Gloucester.

Continue up the road past a stone folly, and along the ridge of common land known as Cud Hill. As the lane bends sharply left, continue on a track alongside the wall to reach the Painswick - Gloucester road. Continue along the verge for 100 yards and then cross to a track on the left. Leave this track within a few yards and climb up to Painswick Beacon, properly called Kimsbury Hill. *A British hill fort occupying a three acre site on the ridge, and bounded to south and east by three tiers of ditches.*

The landscape we walk through in Gloucestershire today is fairly modern and 200 years ago or so the countryside was much wilder and overgrown. The lines of communication were the ancient track ways through the countryside but particularly on the high ground either side of the Severn Vale. First used for movement and migration, the track ways evolved for the transportation of goods and livestock and to connect the habitations and villages that arose, particularly in Anglo-Saxon times. The lines of these old track ways are still largely used today and can be traced clearly on Ordnance Survey maps. Tarmac has overtaken many but other green ways and hidden lanes still exist.

BARBERS BRIDGE - PAINSWICK BEACON

Efforts are being made by National Heritage to discourage further erosion of the summit ridge. These are unlikely to be successful without introducing some form of barriers, and in the long term a boardwalk may be necessary to conserve vulnerable sections of the hillfort. In the meantime it has been suggested that the popular Cotswold Way long distance path be diverted from the summit area. Walkers of the Wysis Way may also care to avoid the badly eroded vicinity of the Trig Point.

Currently being assessed as a National Trail, the Cotswold Way follows the Cotswold escarpment for 100 miles from Chipping Campden in the north of the county, to the Georgian City of Bath. Opened in 1970 the Cotswold Way follows the Cotswold edge, sometimes along it, and at times, descending to the villages tacked under the escarpment before re-climbing the contours. The Cotswold Way joins with the Heart of England Way at Chipping Campden and with the Gloucestershire Way at Crickley Hill.

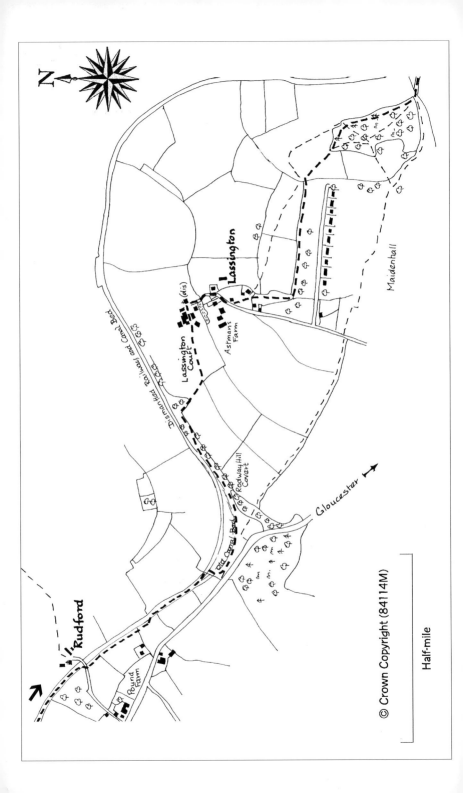

N

Rudford

Round Farm

Dismantled Railway and Canal Bed

Old Canal Bed

Lassington Court

Astman's Farm

Lassington Ct (dis)

Lassington

Roadway Hill Covert

Gloucester

Maidenhall

© Crown Copyright (84114M)

Half-mile

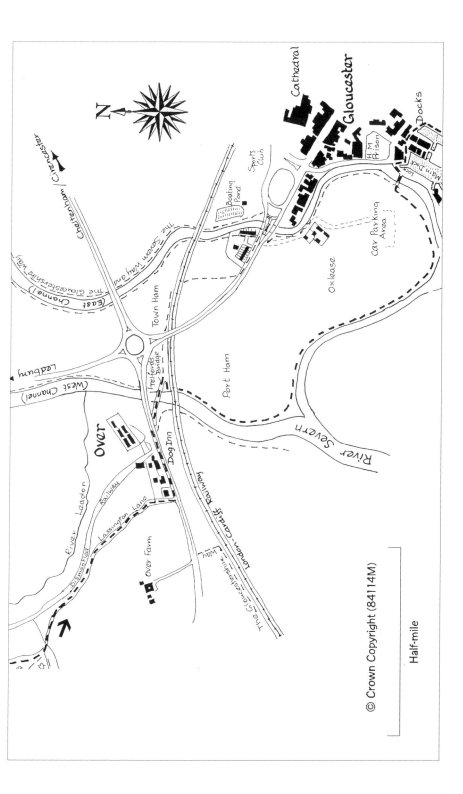

© Crown Copyright (84114M)

Half-mile

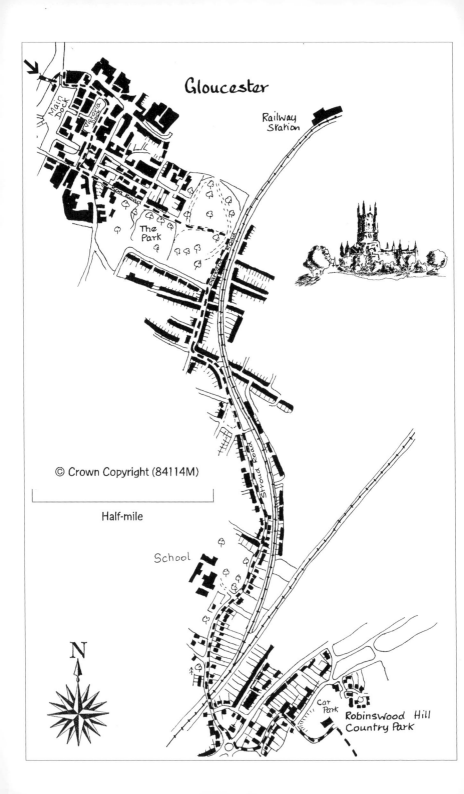

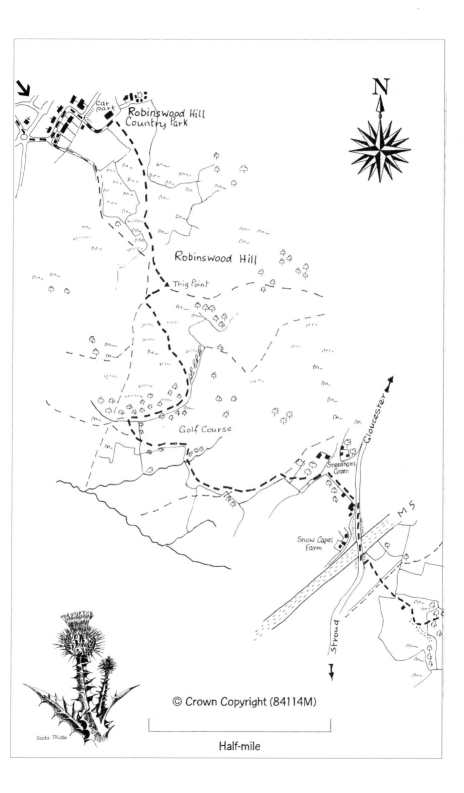

N

Robinswood Hill Country Park

car park

Robinswood Hill

Trig Point

Golf Course

Sneadhams Green

Gloucester

M 5

Snow Capel Farm

Stroud

© Crown Copyright (84114M)

Scots Thistle

Half-mile

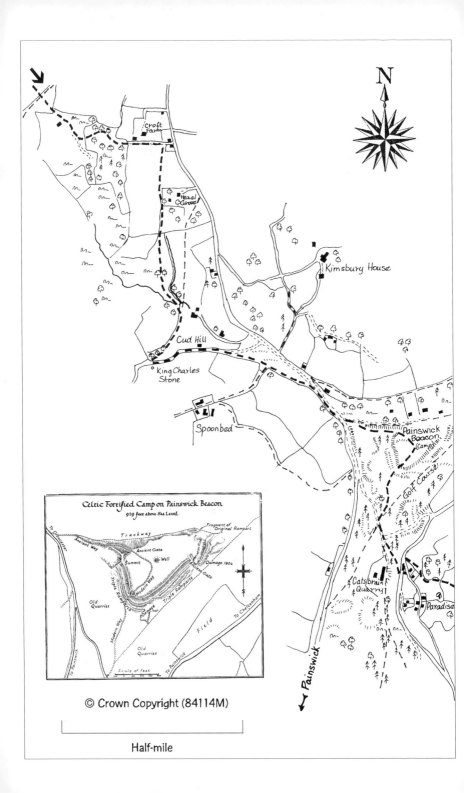

N

Croft Farm

Hazel Grove

Kimsbury House

Cud Hill

King Charles Stone

Spoonbed

Painswick Beacon (Camp)

Golf Course

Cats brain Quarry

Paradise

To Painswick

Celtic Fortified Camp on Painswick Beacon
929 feet above Sea Level.

Fragment of Original Rampart

Trackway

Ancient Gate

To Cheltenham

Ancient Way

Summit

Well

Damage 1904

Ancient Gate

Triple Ramparts

Modern Way

Damage

Triple Ramparts

Old Quarries

Modern Way

Field

To Cheltenham

To Painswick

Old Quarries

Scale of Feet

© Crown Copyright (84114M)

Half-mile

Painswick Beacon - Sapperton

From the Beacon, join the Cotswold Way, an established long distance path, descending to the south along the edge of old quarry workings to join a bridleway crossing the fairway of Painswick Golf Course. After a few yards, turn left on a narrow road to a sharp bend. Leave the Cotswold Way signposted to the right, and instead walk down a footpath through woodland to the Cheltenham - Stroud road and the hamlet of Paradise.

Cross the road to the footway and turn left, passing a house which was once the Adam and Eve Inn. Immediately past the house turn right, down steps, and cross a lane to a footpath along the edge of a garden. Exit by a stone slab stile and turn right down the slope, before curving left around the edge of a wood. Descend to a stile alongside a gate and cross a stream by stepping stones, then a field to a gate into woodland. After only 20 yards or so, turn right, cross two stiles, and walk down a field close to an electricity pole, to a gate and stile. Through these, turn right down to a further gate and stile and cross to yet another stile. Join the farm drive and follow this down to the road and turn left over the Painswick Stream at Damsells Mill.

Woollen mills were built or adapted in every valley possessing a worthwhile head of water. As many as 24 mills once flourished on the Painswick Stream and the spire of Painswick church reflects the prosperity of the mill owners. Competition eventually closed some

53

mills and reduced others to conventional flour milling or to become Pin mills. Several mill buildings nearby remain as private dwellings - Damsells, Lovedays, Brook House, Cap, Kings.

Alongside Damsells Mill turn right onto a footpath, and follow the stream. Cross a side stream by stepping stones and a stile through a hedge and walk down to a junction of streams, footpaths and a bridleway. Do not cross a bridge, but instead turn left and then fork right to follow the bridleway through a gate and up the field beyond.

On the hillside opposite is Painswick Lodge, while to the right, beneath the sheltering fold of Saltridge Hill is the village of Sheepscombe, mentioned in Domesday together with three Shiptons, Yanworth – lamb enclosure, and Sherbourne – clear stream or sheep wash.

After the Roman occupation ended the Saxons deposed the Celts, and their village "Wicke" was later given its name by the local Norman sheriff 'Painfitzjohn'. Painswick Lodge was built in the 15th century by Pains descendants, the Talbots. They became impoverished - not least because of their vicious quarrels with their neighbour Lord Berkeley. The Manorship eventually passed to Sir William Kingston of Miserden who later entertained Henry VIII and Anne Boleyn at Painswick Lodge.

Whether Saltridge Hill was a way used by salt carriers is open to conjecture. When Cotswold was still open country, salt carriers followed prehistoric ways, many of which were later improved by Roman engineers, climbing from the Worcestershire plain over Cotswold by a network of tracks. Deviations from these connected with many of the Manors which owned salt rights at Droitwich. Mediaeval salt carriers were not pioneers in choosing these routes but facing long journeys through wet and wooded country, with

heavily laden animals, they would have used the tracks they found
and which were first trodden out by prehistoric people.

> *Cotswold Choice by Frank Mansell*
> *By Honeycombe and Henley*
> *By Sapperton and Syde*
> *By Climperwell enchanted*
> *Where magic waters bide*
>
> *By Wishanger and Winston*
> *By Camp and Caudle Green*
> *By Battlescombe and Bisley*
> *In quest of love I've been*
>
> *By Miserden and Morcombe*
> *By Stancombe and by Slad*
> *By Eastcombe and by Elcombe*
> *Gay have I gone and sad*
>
> *By Througham Fields and Tunley*
> *By Detcombe and the Dell*
> *By Lypiatt and Longridge*
> *Hang tales too long to tell*
>
> *Oh, Bunnage, Bidfield, Birdlip,*
> *Buckholt and Cranham Knoll*
> *From Paradise to Painswick*
> *At times I've loved them all*
>
> *At times I've loved them all, lad,*
> *But if by chance I die*
> *Then set me down in Sheepscombe*
> *In Sheepscombe I would lie.*

Pass under power lines and close to twin beech trees to a gate in a hedge. The bridleway continues along the contour but the Wysis Way follows an obvious track up the slope ahead. Just before a gate turn right down to a stone slab stile. Drop steeply down the bank to a further stile and then cross the small valley before climbing up to the road in front of a cottage with a castellated roof-line.

Cross the road into a lane and after bending sharply right, step left to the junction of a bridleway and footpath and follow the path to the right, along the wood edge about half a mile. Cross a boundary fence by a massive limestone step and continue behind garden fences to a further stile onto a lane between scattered houses and bungalows. *Clear of the trees, a panorama opens of Painswick, with the church spire prominent, against a background of the ridge between the high points Painswick and Haresfield Beacons.*

Where the houses end, the lane crosses common land, continue for a short distance to a path angling up left through the trees to a road. Ignore a footpath across the road and instead turn right and walk down to Bulls Cross, where old routes to Stroud, Painswick and Sheepscombe meet. From the end of a lay-by area on the left, follow a footpath down the track leading to Trillgate Farm.
Descending, the shapely coppices on Long Ridge Wood and Down Hill rise in front, with the darker outline of Down Wood and The Scrubs beyond. Leave the track and farm buildings by a gate on the left and descend the slope to a stream, then climb the opposite side, curving left and right to a gate onto a track. Turn left, and at the next junction, turn sharp right, and follow this down to join a surfaced lane.

Turn left, and at the lane end take the right fork downhill, passing Down Court, and bending left to Snows Farm. Follow the track to the right, where the footpath leaves abruptly over a stile, and descends the steep hillside to a narrow stone bridge over a stream.

PAINSWICK BEACON TO SAPPERTON

The winding length of The Wysis Way from Sheepscombe is said to be a well known packhorse trail for carrying fleeces from Bisley to Gloucester. The route certainly has the character of an ancient highway and The Woolpack Inn, at nearby Slad, no doubt derives its name from such use.

Native Cotswold sheep produced a thick, heavy fleece, on land which was perfectly suited to them. In mediaeval times Cotswold became the centre of a great wool trade providing England's most important industry for three hundred years. Up to 1500, the wool was mainly exported, but with improving industrial techniques it became efficient for cloth making to be carried out at the source. Cotswold sheep and the mills of the valleys, particularly that of the Frome provided much of England's cloth, as well as great export trade to the continent.

The whole process of breeding and trading sheep and weaving woollen cloth brought great wealth to the Cotswold towns. From Chipping Campden and Northleach to Stroud and Cirencester, many great manor houses and splendid churches were built from some of the proceeds.

Cross the bridge to a stile alongside a gate and follow the path to the right of the hedge, steeply up the lower contours of The Scrubs, and enter the wood through a small gate. *The old track through the wood and, to the right, the deep and wild-looking valley of Piedmont and steep slopes of Keengrove Wood opposite, give an air of timeless antiquity. On a quiet day listen for the jingle of a pack train approaching though the trees!*

Inside the wood the line of the ancient road passes Piedmont Cottage. The right of way has been diverted away from the front of the cottage but at a path junction just beyond, fork left along the front of further cottages and continue directly along the track ahead, still with the valley on your right.

THE WYSIS WAY

Springtime in December

The wind blows chill on Dunkite Hill
But deep below in Dillay,
And all along the valley floor
From Famish Springs to Elcombe,
The Slad Brook pipes an April tune
To bid the stranger welcome.

December on the Bisley Road,
But April in my valley.
Below the darkling Piedmont height
The air is warm in welcome
As evening sunshine turns the hill
To kiss the roofs of Elcombe.

When earth grows cold, and I'm too old
To seek the paths from Dillay,
Then as I dream beside the fire
My glad heart will remember
That there beside the quiet Slad
Is springtime in December.

Arthur Dalby

After about 300 yards, where the track leads to another cottage, turn left and continue along the line of the old road still inside the wood edge. As the valley narrows, the buildings of Sydenhams Farm come into view.

At the valley head, the track bends right and joins a track from the left. Ignore a footpath through a gate to the right, and continue up to a hunt gate at the wood end. Walk up the hollow path beyond to a further gate and then follow the headland to a stile onto the road. Turn right, passing an obsolete Trig point in the field over the wall on the left, and Stancombe

Plantation on the right. At a road junction continue straight over, through a field gate, and along a headland path changing boundaries after a further gate. A short length of enclosed path leads to the Calfway, the road from Birdlip into Bisley.

> *The reason for this name is unclear and may be of fairly recent origin. The earlier name 'calf haga' (calf enclosure), possibly applied to the site of nearby Calfway Farm. However, Chalford, in the nearby Frome valley is said to be 'Calf ford'. The line of the ridgetop road, suggests a good deal more antiquity.*

Turn right and walk into Bisley, where The Bear Inn and The Stirrup Cup can provide welcome refreshment. From the narrow junction of five roads outside the Stirrup Cup, follow an alley to the right. Cross a small road and continue into the churchyard. Walk past the church, and turn left to follow the path alongside the wall and down several flights of steep steps, to a road. Turn right and then follow the road forking left downhill, ignoring left and right turnings. The lane levels and continues down bending left, passing a footpath sign to the right, and becoming a rough twisting track known as Joiners Lane.

Cross a stream where the track becomes a hollow way climbing between hedge banks. After a track joins from the right walk up to a road junction. Cross to a footpath on the right alongside a small barn. Walk up the field to the sky-line, where a stile incorporates an old limestone slab, the first of several similar on this path. Continue to cross two further slab stiles and after a gap in a hedgerow, a slab stile in the boundary on the right. Over this, take the path straight down the field, ignoring a further path following the headland to the right. Cross to a stile in the middle of a curving hedge, where the stone slab has collapsed and is now used as a step.

Walk down the line of two or three trees to a further stile and then descend a steep slope through a small plantation of larches to a further stile. Drop down onto a track and climb a stile into an enclosed path slanting down to the right. After a short distance the path turns left down to a road at Bournes Green.

Cross the small village green and walk down a lane and over a stream in the valley bottom. Continue up the other side for about a 100 yards to a footpath over a slab stile alongside a house. Cross a paddock to a barn and continue along level grassland, *a fine belvedere with views back to Bournes Green and across the valley.*

At the next hedge, fork left up through a higher field to a massive slab stile in the next boundary. Immediately over this, ignore a path straight on but turn right along the line of an ancient green way leading to Oakridge Lynch. Pass through a gate, and turn left to a road. Turn right, with a wall on your right side, and continue alongside the wall to a gate and squeeze stile and walk through to a further gate and stile beyond. The path drops downhill, crossing a small stream by a stone slab and several further stiles, the last of which gives access into Old Hills Wood Nature Reserve.

The path slants downhill to join a track, which leads down to a narrow road in the Frome valley. Turn left to a junction with the Chalford - Frampton Mansell road at Bakers Mill.

The Stroudwater Canal was promoted by clothiers in the Stroud valleys mainly to obtain coal more cheaply than by road. It was completed in 1779 and climbed from the Severn via 13 locks in 8 miles. The canal was able to take Severn trows up to 72 ft. long and 15.5 beam. It ceased to operate in 1941 and was legally abandoned in 1954.

The Thames and Severn Canal was built to connect the two great rivers of England, the Severn and Thames. Engineered by Robert

PAINSWICK BEACON TO SAPPERTON

Whitworth with 28 locks in the 29 miles between Stroudwater and Inglesham lock to the Thames. Opened in 1789, the upper reaches of the canal were never adequately supplied with water which seriously affected the amount of trade and profitability. The section between Chalford and Inglesham was closed in 1927 and the remainder to Stroud in 1933.

The earlier Stroudwater Canal Society became the Stroudwater, Thames and Severn Canal Trust in 1975 and, more recently, the Cotswold Canals Trust. The objective being restoration of both canals in an effort to realise the potential economic value of inland waterways. Apart from the restoration achieved to date, the Trust has significantly contributed to the public debate on the future of the canals, which is currently very optimistic.

Cross the bridge and turn left over a footbridge onto the towpath and follow this scenic length of canal for two miles to Daneway.

The lake behind Bakers Mill was the reservoir supplying lower locks. The juxtaposition of river, canal and railway is a feature of the narrow valley and the viaduct carrying Brunel's Great Western Railway from Swindon is soon in view across the canal.
From the Pucks Mill upper lock, where the towpath changes sides, footpaths lead, in a quarter of a mile, to the Crown Inn at Frampton Mansell.

Approaching the head of the valley, the locks become more numerous and the highest, Bathurst Meadow, Siccaridge Wood Lower, Middle Upper and Daneway Basin, all had 'ponds', still partly visible, in order to conserve enough water to operate the locks.

During the construction of the canal, the Daneway Inn was named the Bricklayers Arms and was the centre for a hive of activity.

Particularly so when the canal was completed up to that point, as the tunnel was still under construction and goods had to be transferred from the canal for road carriage to Cirencester, Lechlade and beyond. Work continued on the tunnel for a further three years, perhaps demonstrating the reason why 'tunnelling wrote indelible lines of worry on many an engineers face.'

Suitably refreshed at the Daneway, continue along the towpath for a short distance until the canal line turns from the valley directly towards the hillside. From the end of the towpath climb behind the tunnel portal to a stile and then walk diagonally up the field towards Sapperton Church. From a stile at the top of the field walk up an enclosed track to Church Lane and turn right to the village street near the school.

> *Legacy*
> *When twice a hundred years have gone*
> *Across my Cotswold eaves,*
> *And still the woods of Sapperton*
> *Make summer of green leaves,*
> *Come then and sing what song you will,*
> *You lovers of new time,*
> *But sometimes on my Cotswold hill*
> *Renew my Cotswold rhyme.*
>
> *John Drinkwater*

Saperton – place of soap makers – probably referring to Fullers Earth used in the treading "walking" of the woollen cloth. Pinsbury Park across the valley, was the home of Sir Robert Atkyns, who wrote Gloucestershire's equivalent of the Doomsday record. His effigy can be found in the church. The poet laureate John Masefield lived for a time at Pinsbury Park, as did later some of the founders of the Guild of Craftsmen in the county. Sapperton was also the home, in 1773, of Charles Mason partly responsible for the peace making

Mason-Dixon Line, in what was to become the United States of America. It is said that the marker stones for the boundary line came from a Gloucestershire quarry.

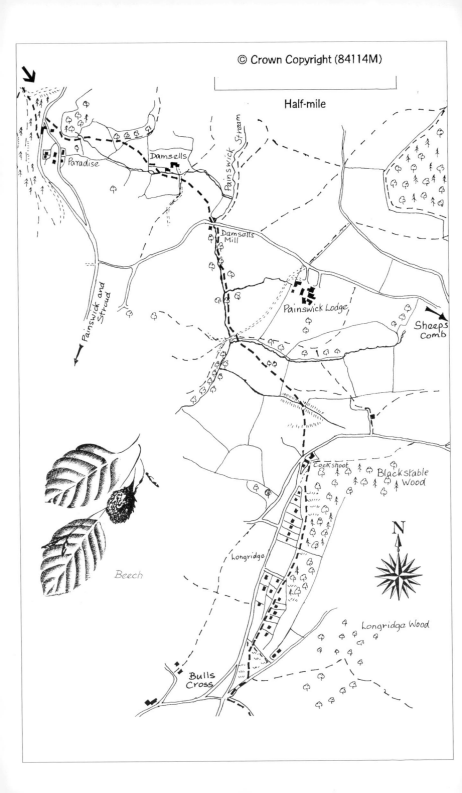

© Crown Copyright (84114M)

Half-mile

Paradise

Damsells

Painswick Stream

Damsells Mill

Painswick Lodge

Painswick and Stroud

Sheeps Comb

Beech

Cockshoot

Blackstable Wood

N

Longridge

Longridge Wood

Bulls Cross

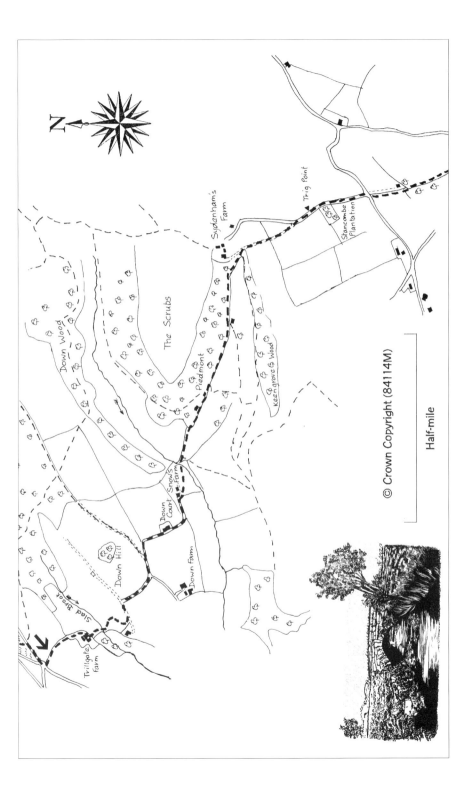

N

© Crown Copyright (84114M)

Half-mile

Down Wood

The Scrubs

Piedmont

Keengrove Wood

Sydenham's Farm

Trig Point

Stancombe Plantation

Down Wood

Down Hill

Down Court

Snow's Farm

Down Farm

Slad Brook

Trillgates Farm

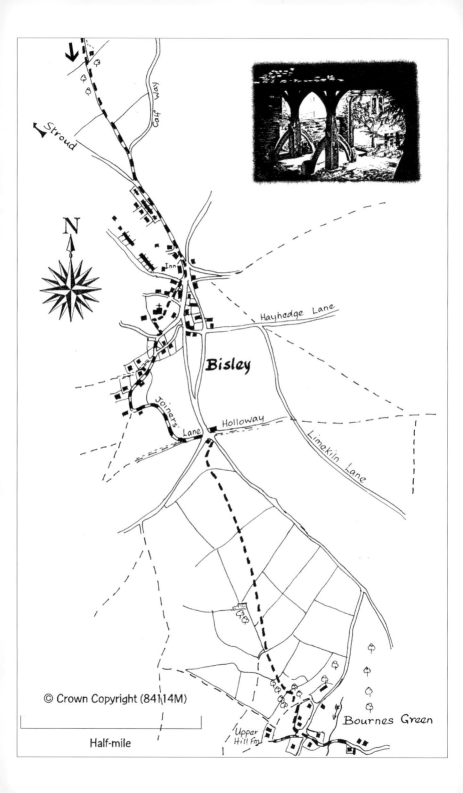

Stroud

Calf way

N

Inn

Hayhedge Lane

Bisley

Joiners Lane

Holloway

Limekiln Lane

© Crown Copyright (841 14M)

Half-mile

Upper Hill Fm

Bournes Green

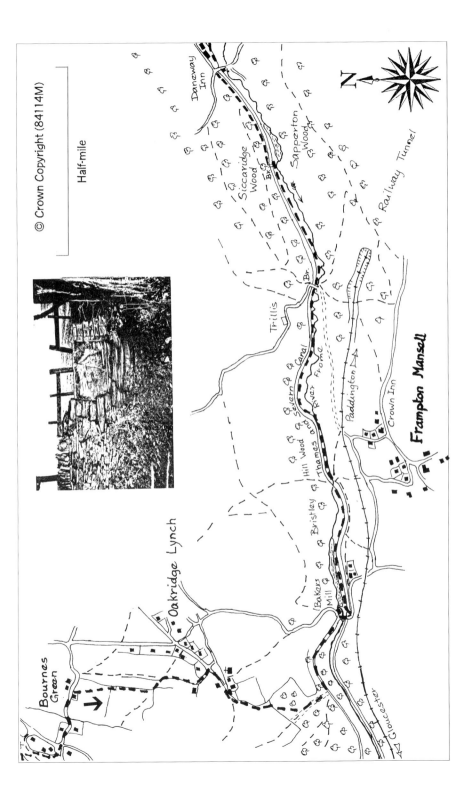

© Crown Copyright (84114M)

Half-mile

N

Daneway Inn

Siccaridge Wood

Sapperton Wood

Railway Tunnel

Br.

Br.

Trillis

Severn Canal

Thames and Severn Canal

River Frome

Hill Wood

Bristley

Paddington

Crown Inn

Frampton Mansell

Bakers Mill

Oakridge Lynch

Bournes Green

Gloucester

Sapperton - Kemble

Cross the road to an alley directly opposite the school and follow this to join a road for about a mile.

For the first half mile, the road approximates to the line of the Sapperton Tunnel and tree-clad mounds show the line of some of the twenty five ventilation shafts which were necessary when the canal was constructed. Note that the trees were not planted with the environment in mind but rather as a cash crop on Canal Company land.

Cross the line of Broad Ride, one of ten radiating out from the centre of Oakley Wood, in Cirencester Park and continue over a crossroad.

Alternative Route
After a further 300 yards, turn right on a footpath through a gate, and cross the field diagonally to the right of a tree covered mound. At the boundary with woodland, a hollow way leads downhill through a wicket gate alongside a horse jump. After 50 yards the stone parapet around Casey Well stands at a path junction. Fork left and continue downhill for a short distance, then along a narrow valley which curves right to join the Stroud-Cirencester road. The footpath straight across the road provides a choice of many permissive ways through Hailey Wood, to reach Tunnel House.

From the crossroads continue along the road for another half mile, before turning right through a squeeze stile in the wall, on a path across the field to the Stroud - Cirencester road.

Cross the road and a field to a hunt gate into Hailey Wood and follow the track into the woodland.
After 200 yards continue over a cross track, and again after 100 yards, cross another of the rides radiating from Cirencester Park.
The woodland track parallels the canal tunnel and airshafts can be seen on the right of the track, surrounded by deer fences. The track curves left, descending over a cross track and joining a track from the left. Continue over a further track, still descending, and join another track from the left, which then curves right through an arch under the railway. Fork left, following the railway embankment, and shortly reach the Tunnel House Inn, *built to cater for the navvies engaged in building the canal tunnel.*

From the Inn, again refreshed, walk down to the eastern portal of the tunnel and follow the towpath for over a mile, passing in succession, under a road bridge, the remains of a Canal Company Roundhouse and under the railway again, to arrive at Coatesfield bridge.

The rebuilding of the eastern portal to the tunnel was one of the first acts of the Canal Trusts. Most of the original stone being recovered from the canal bed Currently, trips are available for about a mile into the tunnel but roof collapse prevents further entry.

Roundhouses are peculiar to the Thames and Severn canal. Provided as accommodation for a lengthsman, the building consists of three stories connected by a curving stairway built into the walls. Some, Roundhouses, as in this instance, had an inverted cone roof to catch and store a supply of rainwater. The railway bridge is imposing and remarkable for the engineering skill of the skewed brickwork

THE WYSIS WAY

From Coatesfield bridge the canal executes a sharp turn and the barge towropes have worn deep grooves in the rubbing stones of the bridge. The towpath is no longer a right of way, but a public path crosses the bridge where paths branch to Coates and Cirencester.

On Buying OS Sheet 163

I own all this. Not loutish acres
That tax the spirit, but the hawking
Eye's freehold, paper country.

 Thirty two inches of aqueduct
Windmill (disused), club house,
embankment,
Public conveniences

In rural areas. This is my
Landlocked landscape that lives in cipher,
And is truer than walking.

Red and imperial, the Romans
Stride eastward. Mysterious, yellow,
The Salt Way halts and is gone.

Here, bigger than the hamlets they are,
Wild wayside syllables stand blooming:
Filkins, Lechlade, Broughton Poggs.

Here only I discard the umber
Reticulations of sad cities,
The pull and drag of mud.
                    U A Fanthorpe.

The Wysis Way turns right, following a track which parallels the canal. Below Tarlton field barn, on the hill to the right, walk through a gateway and along the edge of the wood to alight, suddenly, at the highest source of the Thames, or Isis. Unfortunately, during recent years the water table has fallen leaving the spring almost permanently dry.

A reclining figure, representing either Neptune or Old Father Thames, once graced this isolated spot, but is now at St. John's lock, Lechlade, presumably being more accessible to the cameras of tourists.

The commemorative stone marking the spring bears the legend;

> **The conservators of the River Thames**
> **1857-1974.**
> **This stone was placed here to mark**
> **the source of the River Thames.**

To overcome the feeling of anti-climax at the end of the walk, and disappointment at the lack of water at the source, the short walk with the Thames Path into Kemble, will probably be therapeutic.

The rivers of Cotswold (with one exception), the Coln, Churn, Windrush, Evenlode, Leach and lesser tributaries, flow east to the Thames. The true source is often disputed, but the river, from Trewsbury Mead to the Keynes villages and Lechlade, has been called Isis or Thames for hundreds of years. Springs were once plentiful in the vicinity but, as elsewhere in recent years, the water table has become much lower. The Isbourne, rising on the watershed above Winchcombe flows north and east into Shakespeare's Avon.

THE WYSIS WAY

The Thames Path National Trail meanders for 180 miles to the Thames Barrier at Greenwich. The Wysis Way links the Thames Path to the Offa's Dyke Trail at Monmouth and to the Gloucestershire Way and the Severn Way at Gloucester.

Walk across fields and from the second fieldgate, ignoring a path uphill to the right, continue to a further gate and follow the boundary of a long field to the Tetbury-Cirencester road, the Fosse Way, at Thameshead .

The canal now contours the valley to the left where the Thames Head Wharf once stood. A quarter of a mile to the right along the Fosse is the Thameshead Inn, originally built by the Railway Company as the Great Western Hotel.

Cross the Fosse to a stone slab stile and descend steps alongside a culvert which provides, on occasions, for the flow of the infant Thames. Walk along the valley bottom for a short distance to the line of a watercourse just below a house, hidden by trees on the line of the canal.

The site of Thameshead Pumping Station, where, virtually throughout the life of the canal, water was pumped from a 64 ft. deep well in the effort to keep a sufficient head of water in the canal bed. A succession of pumping engines were used until a second hand Cornish engine was installed in 1854. This increased the pumping capacity to three million gallons a day. The well never ran dry, indicating that although you may not be able to see the Thames, it is, nonetheless, present.

The public footpath slants up, right, to follow the boundary hedge to a gate, from which the line of the path angles down to the river. Most walkers of the Wysis Way will be unable to resist walking directly down for their first sight of the Thames, emerging from the limestone strata on its long meander to Greenwich. If continuing with the Thames Path, follow the stream and cross the road. Otherwise, turn right before the road bridge and follow a footpath, and then a side road, directly to Kemble Railway Station, passing the village post office and shop.

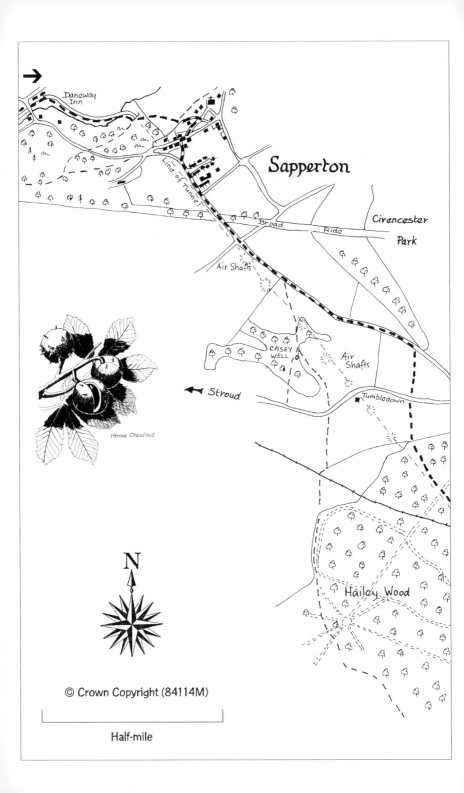

Daneway
Inn

Line of Tunnel

Sapperton

Cirencester
Park

Broad   Ride

Air Shafts

CASEY
WELL

Air
Shafts

◀ Stroud

■ Tumbledown

Horse Chestnut

N

Hailey Wood

© Crown Copyright (84114M)

Half-mile

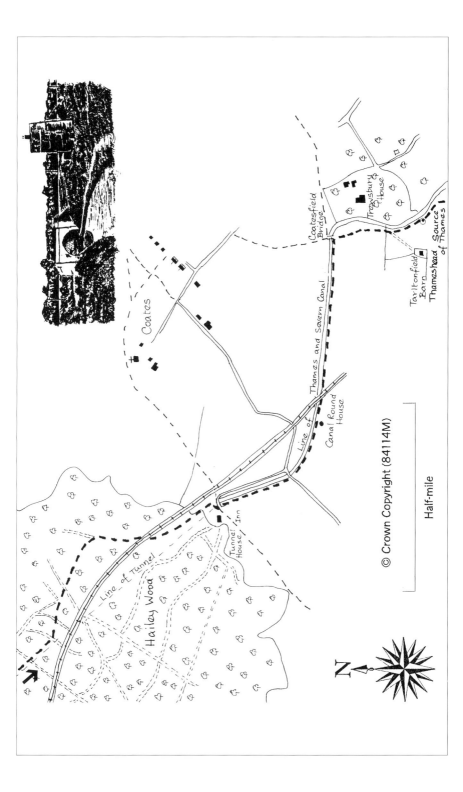

Coates

Line of Thames and Savarn Canal

Coatesfield Bridge

Treasbury House

Tarltonfield Barn

Thameshead Source of Thames

Canal Round House

Line of

Line of Tunnel

Hailey Wood

Tunnel House Inn

© Crown Copyright (84114M)

Half-mile

N

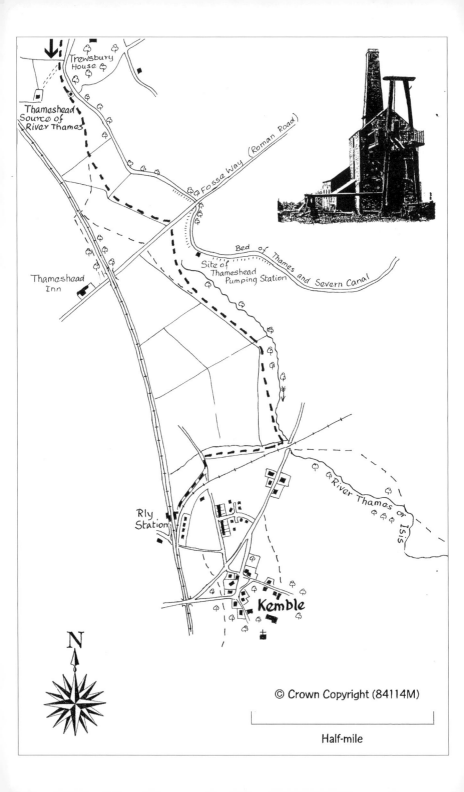

Trewsbury
House

Thameshead
Source of
River Thames

Fosse Way (Roman Road)

Bed of Thames and Severn Canal

Site of
Thameshead
Pumping Station

Thameshead
Inn

River Thames or Isis

Rly.
Station

Kemble

N

© Crown Copyright (84114M)

Half-mile

Mileages

Monmouth:

Hillersland	5 1/4	5 1/4
Carters Piece	1 3/4	7
Nailbridge	5	**12**
Mitcheldean	3	15
May Hill	3 1/2	18 1/2
Glasshouse	1 1/2	20
Tibberton	3 1/2	23 1/2
Barbers Bridge	1	**24 1/2**
Gloucester	5 1/2	30
Robinswood Hill	3	33
Sneedhams Green	1 1/2	34 1/2
Painswick Beacon	2 1/2	**37**
Sheepscombe	2	39
Bisley	4	43
Bournes Green	1.5	44 1/2
Daneway	3	47 1/2
Sapperton	0 1/2	**48**
Tunnel House	2 1/2	50 1/2
Thames Head	1 1/4	51 3/4
Kemble	2	**53 3/4**

Tourist Information Centres

Monmouth Tourist Information Centre,
Shire Hall, Agincourt Square. 01600 713899

Chepstow Tourist Information Centre,
Castle Car Park, Bridge Street. 01291 623772

Coleford Tourist Information Centre,
27 Market Place. 01594 836307

Newent Tourist Information Centre,
The Library, High Street. 01531 822145

Gloucester Tourist Information Centre,
St. Michael's Tower, The Cross. 01452 421188

Painswick Tourist Information Centre,
The Library, Stroud Road. 01452 813552

Stroud Tourist Information Centre,
Subscription Rooms, George Street. 01453 765768

Cirencester Tourist Information Centre,
Corn Hall Market Place. 01285 654180

Swindon Tourist Information Centre,
37 Regent Street. 01793 530328

Faringdon Tourist Information Centre,
7a Market Place. 01367 242191

Oxford Tourist Information Centre,
St Aldates Chambers. 01865 726871